# CLASS 56 LOCOMOTIVES

John Dedman, Steve Clark
and
Mark Finch

AMBERLEY

*Front Cover*: A shot now consigned to history with the closure of Hatfield Colliery in 2015; work-stained No. 56073 *Tremorfa Steelworks* snakes out of Hatfield Colliery with an unidentified MGR working. 25 May 2000 (MF)

*Rear cover from top to bottom*:

Transrail No. 56064 works a late-running 6D51 Doncaster Belmont to Hull Enterprise, conveying one BYA coil wagon and a variety of tanks destined for Melton Lane (Ferriby). 25 June 1999. (MF)

EWS-liveried No. 56037 passes through Grangetown with the 7G55 from Redcar conveying limestone in hooded HBA wagons destined for Shap Quarry. 31 March 2003. (MF)

Romanian-built No. 56012 is going north at Clay Cross Junction on 4 July 1985 with a rake of empty HAA coal hoppers. The first thirty of the 135 Class 56s were built in Romania; the remainder were built at BR Works at Doncaster and Crewe. (JD)

On 30 July 1985, No. 56047 has charge of the 7V85 12.32 Fareham to Westbury empty stone wagons, the first of which has not been emptied for some reason. These PTA wagons were originally in iron ore service and when made redundant they were transferred to aggregate traffic. No. 56047 is passing the English China Clays quarry at East Grimstead, which is nearing the end of its working life; it is still there as of 2017, but totally overgrown. (JD)

First published 2018

Amberley Publishing
The Hill, Stroud
Gloucestershire, GL5 4EP

www.amberley-books.com

Copyright © John Dedman, Steve Clark and Mark Finch, 2018

The right of John Dedman, Steve Clark and Mark Finch to be identified as the Authors of this work has been asserted in accordance with the Copyrights, Designs and Patents Act 1988.

ISBN 978 1 4456 6176 6 (print)
ISBN 978 1 4456 6177 3 (ebook)

British Library Cataloguing in Publication Data.
A catalogue record for this book is available from the British Library.

Typesetting by Amberley Publishing.
Printed in the UK.

# Introduction

An oil crisis in the early 1970s prompted BR to hastily think about investing in a new Type 5 freight loco capable of hauling vast tonnages of coal from pit to power station using the relatively new MGR (merry-go-round) concept. The go ahead was given by the government and plans to build what would be known as the Class 56 locomotives began. Deliveries of the class began from 1976, with the first batch of thirty being built by Electroputere in Romania. These were followed by eighty-five built at Doncaster and twenty built at Crewe, making a total of 135 locos, completed in 1984. To give a chance for Doncaster to get their production line ready the initial batch was built abroad; however, the workmanship left a lot to be desired and all thirty locos had to be extensively re-worked to make them serviceable. All locos were designed for freight use and were fitted with air brakes only. Railway privatisation from the late 1980s onwards meant that these locos changed ownership many times and, consequently, they wore a number of different liveries, as illustrated within these pages.

Freight traffic covered includes coal, steel, petroleum, stone, engineers and mixed wagonload freight, but there will be the odd passenger train and railtour, for which the Class 56s were always a popular choice.

During their BR careers the Class 56s were blighted by reliability problems, and these prompted the likes of Foster Yeoman to look to the USA for motive power in the shape of the Class 59. However, the first real nail in the coffin came when the Class 60s started rolling off the production line at Brush Works, Loughborough, allowing some of the poorer examples of the Grids to be taken out of traffic to provide some much needed spares. The class continued through to the late 1990s without many inroads being made but all that was to change when a Canadian Company, Wisconsin Central Transport Corporation, was to take over freight operations from Mainline, Loadhaul and Transrail. The newly formed company was to be known as the English, Welsh & Scottish Railway, or EWS for short, and with it came an order for 250 new Class 66 locos. The first of these locos appeared on our shores in 1998 and were displayed to the general public at the Toton open day in August of that year. Despite a rousing speech from MD Ed Burkhardt, saying that our 'heritage locos' would be around for a while yet, I think most of us knew it was the beginning of the end. The race was now on to record these (and other locos) before they disappeared from the main line.

Almost as soon as a boatload of 66s arrived, a batch of Class 37s, 56s or 58s was put into storage. Many thought that the newer 58s would outlast the older Class 56s, but that was not to happen.

From 2000 onwards, some Class 56s led a charmed life, with several machines going in and out of storage like a yo-yo, but the class clung on to several key workings such as the Scunthorpe coal circuit and the Boulby to Tees Dock potash workings. Ironically, Class 56 reliability got better towards the end of their working lives thanks to modifications made at Brush Works, Loughborough, and at places like Immingham and Toton TMD.

With a further change in ownership and management within EWS, the bean counters deemed that the Class 56s would be withdrawn at the end of the 2003/2004 financial year, meaning that March 2004 was going to be 'The End'. And so it was on 31 March 2004 that No. 56115 started off from Bristol Temple Meads with Pathfinder's 'Twighlight Grid' railtour. No. 56078 joined in the fun at York, working a circular tour around the Pennines, before both 56s headed the tour back to Bristol from York. I was present among a huge gallery at Burton Salmon, near Knottingley, to witness what many thought was the last time we would see a Class 56 on Network Rail metals. History, however, tells us otherwise.

In 2005, several Class 56s and 58s were re-activated and made their way through the Channel Tunnel to work for French-based infrastructure company Fertis, working ballast trains on a newly constructed high-speed line between Paris and Strasbourg.

If that wasn't enough, Jarvis announced it was setting up in the locomotive hire business and wanted Grids to haul trains for its Fastline Freight operation and, subsequently, Nos 56301, 302 and 303 appeared on the main line in 2005. Hanson Traction returned a further two Grids to the main line as Nos 56311 and 56312, the latter in a garish purple livery and named *Artemis*.

Since then we have had Colas, who currently have ten Grids on their books, Devon & Cornwall Railway (DCR), who have five, and Rail Operations Group (ROG), who have fifteen, so the Grids are still clinging on. Quite what the future holds for these locos is anyone's guess but you can bet that wherever a Class 56 goes, someone will be there with a camera or camcorder to record that movement on film.

The book spans the years from 1980 to 2017 and is arranged in approximate date order to show the progression of the class through the years as they have moved to and from different areas with different liveries and owners. This is by no means a definitive history of the class, showing all geographical areas worked or every train worked by the class, but it is a good representation of the core workings that these locos were to be seen on.

With all three authors living on the South Coast, many miles were driven up and down the country's motorways to capture these locos on film, so when John suggested doing this book with Amberley Publishing, both Mark and myself jumped at the chance. We just hope we've done the class justice.

Steve Clark

No. 56051 is heading north at Loughborough with a train of empty flyash wagons on 13 June 1980. It is the 6M46 15.35 from Fletton to Ratcliffe Power Station. The flyash wagons look very similar to the CPV cement pressflos, but are larger wagons and coded CSA. (JD)

Romanian-built No. 56034 is at Fairwood Junction on 6 June 1984 with Yeoman and Tilcon loaded PGA stone hoppers. This loco was named *Castell Ogwr/Ogmore Castle* in 1985, after the castle near Bridgend in Glamorgan. (JD)

On a windy 5 September 1984, another Romanian-built classmember is seen – No. 56033 with loaded Yeoman PGA hoppers. It is 6O63, the 08.15 Westbury to Botley, passing East Grimstead. (JD)

No. 56047 heads a train of 4SUB units from Eastleigh, heading for a scrapyard in South Wales on 5 September 1984. (JD)

During 1985 the Eastleigh to Severn Tunnel Junction Speedlink was booked for a Class 45 loco. This was regularly substituted by a Class 47 but on 8 March a very grubby No. 56058 was in charge. It is seen here as it was departing from Eastleigh with a good load consisting of BDAs, an SPA, HEAs and a selection of MOD wagons on the rear. (JD)

No. 56033 is seen arriving at Eastleigh with the 6O81 10.03 Merehead Quarry to Eastleigh loaded Yeoman PGA stone hoppers on 19 April 1985. The train is arriving from the freight-only route from Romsey via Chandlers Ford. Passenger trains have since been re-introduced on this route. (JD)

Large logo, blue-liveried No. 56128 was a surprise turn up on the Severn Tunnel Junction to Eastleigh Speedlink at East Grimstead on 30 July 1985. Behind the loco are a good mix of MOD wagons, including Warwell, VEA, OBA, VDA and Warflat with some TTA tanks bringing up the rear. No. 56128 was later repainted into Railfreight coal sector livery, followed by Transrail livery. It eventually became part of the Devon & Cornwall Railway (DCR) fleet but was not put into service, instead being used as a source of spare parts. (JD)

Large logo-liveried No. 56084 has just arrived at Westbury with loaded tarmac PGA hoppers. The first and seventh wagons are ex-bulk salt PGAs. No. 56084 was later painted into coal sector livery, followed by Loadhaul livery. Sister loco No. 56048 is seen in the depot surrounded by various Class 47s and 56s in standard blue livery on 11 May 1985. (JD)

Brand-new in BR blue large logo livery, No. 56133 *Crewe Locomotive Works* is seen in the Crewe Works yard on 22 July 1984. No. 56133 was put into service a week later and was finally withdrawn in 2004. (JD)

Weekend visits to Barrow Hill Depot always produced some Class 56s, and 22 September 1984 was no exception, with three large logo-liveried examples lined up outside the shed – Nos 56120, 56108 and 56085. (JD)

Barrow Hill Depot building was a roundhouse with the storage lines fed from a turntable. BR blue-liveried No. 56016 was inside the building on 22 September 1984. Barrow Hill is a former Midland Railway roundhouse and is now used as a base for preserved diesel locos by various preservation groups; special events including steam and diesel galas are held here every year. No. 56016 only lasted until 1992 when it was withdrawn from service and used as a source for spares. (JD)

Clipstone Junction is the location for this view of Romanian-built No. 56004 heading towards Shirebrook with a loaded MGR train. This loco suffered serious collision damage to both cab ends in 1982. It was rebuilt with British style ends and re-entered service in 1984, which is probably why it still looks ex-works in this view taken on 3 July 1985. (JD)

Shirebrook was a busy location for coal trains in the 1980s, and No. 56024 is seen heading north with an empty MGR train on 3 July 1985. The remains of the original station platforms can be seen either side of the tracks, and the 1965-built diesel depot, which closed in 1996, is in the background. The station was re-opened in 1998 as part of the Robin Hood line. (JD)

Passing the signal box and semaphores at Shirebrook is No. 56115 with a southbound empty MGR on 3 July 1985. No. 56115 is one of three of the class now in service with Floyd in Hungary; the other two are Nos 56101 and 56117. (JD)

No. 56106 is heading south at Whitwell on 3 July 1985 with an empty MGR train. Subsequent liveries for this loco were Railfreight coal, Loadhaul and Fertis. It is still in the Fertis livery in 2017 and is owned and stored by UK Rail Leasing. (JD)

First of its class, No. 56001 is heading along the single track near Crampmoor with the 6V81 16.00 Eastleigh to Merehead Quarry empty Yeoman PGA stone hoppers on 13 September 1985. In 1987 this was the first Class 56 to receive Railfreight sector livery. (JD)

After a shower of rain on 7 May 1986, No. 56038 *Western Mail* is approaching Newport with a trainload of steel slabs on BDA wagons. No. 56038 was allocated to Cardiff Canton Depot and named at Cardiff station in June 1981 after the city's morning newspaper by its editor. (JD)

No. 56040 *Oystermouth* and No. 56032 *Sir De Morgannwg/County of South Glamorgan* are heading west near Marshfield with empty iron ore tipplers from Llanwern to Port Talbot on 25 April 1986. No. 56032 is now owned by UK Rail Leasing; it is in Fertis livery and is stored at Leicester. (JD)

No. 56051 in early Railfreight grey livery and No. 56040 *Oystermouth* in BR blue livery, with a loaded iron ore service from Port Talbot to Llanwern Steelworks, are seen near Marshfield on 7 May 1986. No. 56051 is now owned by Colas Rail and is stored at Washwood Heath. No. 56040 was preserved by the Class 56 Group but was sold for scrap in 2012 when they replaced it with No. 56301, which was in much better condition. (JD)

BR blue pair Nos 56052 and 56001 are seen approaching Newport with a loaded iron ore service from Port Talbot to Llanwern Steelworks on 7 May 1986. (JD)

No. 56056 is heading east near Marshfield with fifteen 100-ton bogie tanks on 25 April 1986. No. 56056 was in service from 1979 to 2004, when it was withdrawn as surplus to requirements. (JD)

Romanian-built Class 56 No. 56020 has charge of the 7V46 10.12 Toton Old Bank to Didcot Power Station loaded MGR coal train. It is approaching Wichnor Junction on 19 June 1986. This busy location produced a very varied selection of locos and types of freight trains. (JD)

The Westbury to Totton ARC stone train is being unloaded in Eling Yard on 12 June 1986. No. 56039 has split the train into two portions in Totton Yard and, as can be seen, each portion is propelled through the unloader. The loaded train arrives as the 6O53 Tuesday and Thursday-only 09.10 from Westbury and departs as the 6V31 14.35 from Totton. (JD)

No. 56006 in Railfreight grey is heading north at Shirebrook with empty HAA hoppers on 15 July 1986. This loco was finally withdrawn from service by EWS in 2003 and was eventually saved for preservation with the Class 56 Group at Leicester. (JD)

No. 56029 has just passed Shirebrook Depot with a loaded MGR on 15 July 1986. At the depot are Class 08, 20, 37, 56 and 58 locos. The line diverging from the right of the depot is the branch to Warsop Colliery. In the distance on the right are a pair of Class 20s on the line to Clipstone Junction and more collieries, all of which are now closed. (JD)

No. 56107 in large logo blue livery heads a northbound empty MGR at Clay Cross on 16 July 1986. (JD)

An unusual combination of No. 56118 and No. 37095 depart south from Toton Yard with the 6M29 23.00 Lackenby BSC to Corby BSC steel coil on 16 July 1986. The train had arrived from the north triple-headed, with the Class 56 heading Nos 37159 and 37095. No. 37159 appeared to have a fault as it was removed to the diesel depot. No. 37095 was named *British Steel Teeside* the previous October, although in 1987 the name was transferred to the refurbished No. 37502. (JD)

No. 56060 is running along the sea wall on the Towy Estuary at Ferryside with empty 100-ton tanks destined for Waterstone or Robeston Sidings on 3 July 1987. This loco is today part of the UK Rail Leasing fleet and is stored. (JD)

BR blue-liveried No. 56071 is heading south from Stenson Junction with a set of empty HAA wagons on 7 September 1987. The tracks on the right lead into the coal-fired Willington Power Station, which closed in 1999. There are now proposals to build a gas power station on the site. (JD)

No. 56091 is heading south at Treeton Junction on the outskirts of Sheffield on 7 July 1987 with a short coal train consisting of three HEA wagons and three coal containers. No. 56091 is still around in 2017 and is owned by British American Railway Services in Fertis livery. (JD)

On 3 July 1988, Nos 56019 and 56025 are stabled at Worksop for the weekend. No. 56019 is in Railfreight grey livery with the red stripe around the base of the body and No. 56025 is still in its original standard blue livery. (JD)

In matching large logo livery, consecutively numbered Nos 56110 and 56109 are at Knottingley Depot on 3 July 1988. (JD)

No. 56134 *Blyth Power* is in coal sector livery but without depot plaques. It is seen at South Bank with a loaded MGR from Immingham to Scunthorpe Steelworks on 4 July 1988. (JD)

No. 56042 has charge of a southbound loaded MGR at Clay Cross Junction on 6 July 1988. This loco was fitted with CP1 bogies – a prototype for the CP3 bogies that were fitted to the Class 58s. (JD)

Heading west from Newport on 28 October 1988 are No. 56044 in Railfreight red stripe livery and No. 56031 *Merehead* in BR blue livery with iron ore PTA wagons. (JD)

No. 56028 *West Burton Power Station* is passing Toton Yard and TMD with an empty MGR on 8 July 1989. Plenty of Class 20s can be seen in the depot, which also has Class 08, 31 and 56 locos plus the depot breakdown train. (JD)

In the new Railfreight coal livery, No. 56028 *West Burton Power Station* with a loaded MGR is seen at Shipley in the Erewash Valley on 8 July 1989. (JD)

In original Railfreight grey livery, No. 56043 is at Salisbury with empty Tiger Rail POA wagons from Botley, returning to Westbury on 12 October 1989. (JD)

Railfreight petroleum-liveried No. 56036 is seen at Salisbury on 12 October 1989 with an eastbound stone train from Westbury made up of ARC PTA wagons. (JD)

No. 56055 in Railfreight construction livery is seen at Westbury with a set of ARC PGA hoppers on 5 April 1990. (JD)

No. 56135 *Port of Tyne Authority* is heading north at Winwick with the 6E23 20.37 Ellesmere Port to Blyth Dock Cawoods coal containers when seen on 13 June 1990. (JD)

On 1 July 1990, British Rail ran the Gloucester 150 Rail Day to celebrate 150 years of Gloucester's railways. As well as the many locomotives and other attractions that were on display, Pathfinder ran trains between Birmingham and Bristol hauled by Nos 20084 and 20170, Nos 20096 and 20025, Nos 37100 and 37074, Nos 37691 and 37800, and Nos 56034 and 58004. No. 56034 *Castell Ogwr/Ogmore Castle* is seen near Gloucester with the 08.25 from Bristol Temple Meads. (JD)

No. 56048 is seen heading east towards Newport with three VAA vans on 27 September 1990. (JD)

One of a batch of Grids based in the North East at Gateshead, No. 56131 *Ellington Colliery* is seen recently outshopped in Trainload coal livery. It shares Blyth Cambois Depot with other members of the class and a solitary Class 37 in 1990. (SC)

Being nominally a freight-only loco, the Class 56s were popular choices for railtours, which gave the haulage men a chance for more red lines in the book. In the early 1990s, DC Tours ran a series of tours on Southern metals entitled the Solent and Wessex Wanderers. Railfreight grey-liveried No. 56019 was used on tour number 4 between Eastleigh and Weymouth, and the Grid is seen awaiting departure from the seaside town with the return working on 26 January 1992. (SC)

No. 56036 was already a bit of a celebrity loco, having been the first of its class to gain the large logo livery. When the 56s were painted in the 'Trainload' liveries, No. 56036 was the only member of the class to gain petroleum decals, as seen here in this shot taken at Hither Green Depot in 1992. This loco also became one of the first to wear Dutch livery for infrastructure work based in the South East. (SC)

Toton Depot was always an eagerly anticipated visit on society tours as the depot could boast up to 100 locos on shed at the weekend. In this view in 1992, Nos 56064 and 56059 receive attention to their bogies alongside No. 58046. (SC)

The late 1980s and early 1990s were full of opportunities for spotters and enthusiasts to visit depots and works thanks to society visits and a vast number of open days organised by BR. One such event was held at Worksop's Trainload Coal Depot, and No. 56095 *Harworth Colliery* welcomes visitors to its cab on a sunny 5 September 1993. (SC)

No. 56038 *Western Mail* is heading west at Newport with six Powell Duffryn steel wagons on 16 March 1993. This loco is still around today, although it is stored by UK Rail Leasing at Leicester. (JD)

No. 56115 is powering through Newport station with an MGR made up of HFA coal hoppers on 26 May 1994. (JD)

No. 56133 *Crewe Locomotive Works* is seen at Stratford with the 6L76 21.06 Ditton to Ipswich BOC tanks on 18 August 1994. (JD)

BR blue livery was a rare commodity on the privatised railway; however, some locos did manage to retain it, such as No. 56004, which is seen here in the yard at Bescot with the St Blazey to Cliffe Vale 'Tiger Rail' china clay working in 1995. (SC)

No. 56133 *Crewe Locomotive Works* is seen with 6S79, the 20.05 Arpley Yard to Mossend empty timber OTA wagons, approaching Warrington on 7 June 1995. (JD)

No. 56070 is seen heading south at Warrington at 16.07 on 7 June 1995 with seven TTA chemical tanks; the two blue ones carry sulphuric acid and the white ones caustic soda. (JD)

No. 56119 is passing through Warrington with 6V23, the 15.37 Hardendale Quarry to Margam Limestone CBA covered hoppers, 7 June 1995. (JD)

No. 56029 is seen heading south, passing straight through Crewe station with Shell TTA tanks on 8 June 1995. No. 56029 is in Railfreight sector livery with no sector logos but it has got the Toton Power Station Depot crest on the cabside. (JD)

Catching the last rays of light, Loadhaul No. 56084 approaches Barnetby with a very lightly loaded 6D28 Knottingley TMD to Lindsey traction gas tanks on 12 July 1995. (MF)

Unbranded Loadhaul No. 56130 *Wardley Opencast* heads for home to the North East, passing Monk Fryston with a lengthy rake of HEA wagons conveying coal from Wintersett to Tyne Yard on 15 June 1995. (MF)

Trainload coal-liveried No. 56126 approaches Wrawby Junction with the 6G85 Neville Hill to Lindsey short wheelbase 45-ton tanks, conveying empty gas oil and bitumen from Hunslet East on 12 July 1995. (MF)

Grey day, grey train, as Transrail No. 56114 *Maltby Colliery* pauses at Didcot Parkway with a uniform rake of Transrail HEA wagons forming the 6B20 West Drayton to Coedbach on 7 December 1995. (MF)

Romanian-built pair Nos 56018 and 56010, both in Transrail livery, are seen at Newport on 8 August 1996 with loaded iron ore tipplers from Port Talbot to Llanwern Steelworks. No. 56018 became part of the Fertis fleet and is now owned and stored by UK Rail Leasing. (JD)

The rollercoaster of privatisation took another step for the three freight companies when an American company, Wisconsin Central, decided to buy the assets of Mainline, Transrail and Loadhaul plus RES. This meant yet another livery change for the class. However, with a final livery yet to be decided on, some locos were outshopped in just a white undercoat, as seen here on No. 56096 at Doncaster in 1996. This particular loco was due to be the first in the new red and gold EWS livery; however, it failed on the Doncaster Works test train and its place in the queue was taken by No. 56089. Thanks to Keith Bulmer for the additional information. (SC)

With new kids on the block EWS entering the freight market and no livery finalised at the time, any loco going through the works for overhaul was released in ghost white. One of these was No. 56068, which is seen approaching Knabbs Bridge with a loaded MGR from Immingham to Scunthorpe Steelworks on 3 June 1996 (MF)

Loadhaul power in the form of No. 56006 *Ferrybridge C Power Station* thunders through Barnetby with the 6G40 Hartlepool to Immingham train conveying large-diameter steel pipes on 25 July 1996. This was a short-term contract during the summer of 1996 for a new gas pipeline. (MF)

By the mid-1990s the Trainload liveries were starting to disappear as the three freight companies, Transrail, Mainline and Loadhaul, wanted to personalise their own locomotives. The most striking livery had to be the Loadhaul livery, as seen worn by a very clean No. 56035 at Peterborough on 27 April 1996. The loco had been based at Cardiff and Bristol Bath Road for most of its early career but was now part of Immingham's Loadhaul allocation. (SC)

Transrail-liveried No. 56115 is heading south at Coppenhall near Crewe with 6V23, the 16.18 Hardendale to Margam loaded limestone, on 11 July 1997. The first wagon is an ex-grain polybulk in Distillers livery, which is almost unrecognizable under a layer of limestone dust. The remaining wagons are CBA hoppers. (JD)

The final member of the class, No. 56135 *Port of Tyne Authority*, is seen at Coppenhall, Crewe, on 20 August 1997 in Railfreight livery and has lost its cabside depot plaque but retains its red nameplate. It is in charge of 6H33, the 14.00 Widnes to Earles Sidings cement made up of twenty Metalair PCA bulk cement wagons. (JD)

Former North East coal sector No. 56131 *Ellington Colliery* is signal checked on the approach to Stenson Junction before taking the route across to Sheet Stores with the 6E21 Baglan Bay to Humber pressure tanks on 22 April 1997. (MF)

Unbranded triple grey No. 56108 thunders past Sandiacre with a lengthy rake of Seacows forming the 7E77 Mountsorrel to Doncaster ballast on 28 May 1997. (MF)

In Loadhaul livery, No. 56112 *Stainless Pioneer* is seen heading south at Coppenhall with nine HEA coal hoppers on 11 August 1998. (JD)

Summer Saturdays were a favourite, as anything went when it came to covering for the poor availability of Virgin 47/8s. Romanian Grid No. 56019 in Railfreight red stripe livery ventured to the South Coast, and is seen here at sunny Bournemouth with the 1O38 Edinburgh to Bournemouth on 20 June 1998. (MF)

Loadhaul No. 56085 passes Stenson and slows for the signal at North Staffs Junction with the 6M13 Tees Yard to Etruria steel empties, conveying BDA and spacer wagons, on 22 May 1998. (MF)

Passing over Womersley level crossing at Knottingley East, Romanian Grid No. 56021 rescues No. 09021, which had disgraced itself while working the Sudforth Lane to Knottingley MGR cripples on 29 April 1998. (MF)

Aire Valley native No. 56075 *West Yorkshire Enterprise* storms through Knottingley East with an unidentified coal working bound for Eggborough or Drax Power Station on 29 April 1998. (MF)

A broadside study of No. 56133 *Crewe Locomotive Works* shows just how grubby these locos could get, with the dirt almost masking the 'TRANSRAIL' lettering on the bodyside. The Grid leaves Godfrey Road stabling point and heads for nearby Aleaxandra Dock Junction to work the 6M17 Enterprise freight to Wembley Yard in 1998. This loco lost its nameplates in 2000 and was disposed of by EMR at Kingsbury in 2012. (SC)

With a changeover of crew, Dutch-liveried Transrail No. 56049 makes a fine sight at Warrington Bank Quay with a loaded MGR destined for Fiddlers Ferry Power Station on 14 April 1999. (MF)

Totally unexpected and nearly capturing the photographer by surprise, this triple-headed working at Aldwarke Junction of No. 56112 *Stainless Pioneer* with Nos 56051 and No. 58024 dead in tow was heading an unidentified MGR on 29 June 1999. (MF)

A Grid under pressure as No. 56058 makes haste powering through Warrington Bank Quay with the 6E05 Stanlow to Humber pressure tanks on 4 August 1999. (MF)

EWS-liveried No. 56058 heads through Stenson with a very lengthy 6E08 Wolverhampton to Scunthorpe conveying a variety of empty steel wagons on 25 May 1999. (MF)

Class 56s occasionally pitched up on car trains from the Midlands as it was a simple out and back diagram. No. 56065 slows for a crew change at Eastleigh with a Southampton Eastern Docks to Bordersley train of empty cartics in February 2000. (SC)

With No. 56131 ticking over out of shot, emitting a smoky haze, No. 56069 *Wolverhampton Steel Terminal* snakes out of Arpley Yard across the main line at Warrington Bank Quay conveying a rake of autoballasters on an unidentified engineers' working on 25 March 2000. (MF)

A Grid under the wires as No. 56119 approaches Doncaster with a mixed rake of HAA and Anglo-Scottish HBA hooded wagons on this unidentified coal working on 16 May 2000. (MF)

Transrail-liveried No. 56056, snaking across the pointwork at Doncaster, makes light work of the Drax Power Station to Renishaw MGR empties on 16 August 2000. (MF)

Making hard work of the gradient all the way from Wrawby Junction, No. 56051 passes the fine array of semaphores at Melton Ross with the 6D42 Eggborough Power Station to Lindsey tanks on 17 August 2000. (MF)

Passing a rural-looking Melton Ross, No. 56117 has No. 60096 dead in tow on the daily 6D65 Doncaster Belmont to Immingham Enterprise on 12 September 2000. (MF)

No. 56096 was one of only ten locos to receive the EWS version of the livery before a modified version was decided on. One of several Enterprise trains that headed to and from Humberside served the Potter Group Terminal at Selby and this is the 6D93 return working to Immingham at Wrawby Junction in February 2000. (SC)

Loadhaul No. 56055 creeps up the relief lines at Wrawby Junction, passing the fine array of semaphore signals with MGR empties from Scunthorpe Steelworks to Immingham on 29 March 2001. (MF)

Minus the big 'T' Transrail logo, No. 56054 *British Steel Llanwern* has the peg for the Scunthorpe line at Wrawby Junction with another load of black gold destined for Scunthorpe Steelworks on 3 March 2001. (MF)

No. 56103 *Stora* passes Brocklesby station with a loaded MGR train for the furnaces at Scunthorpe Steelworks. The loco will need all of its 3,250 hp to lift its heavy train up the gradient through Croxton towards Melton Ross before coasting down towards Barnetby on 16 August 2001. (SC)

EWS-liveried No. 56089 comes off the Lincoln line at Wrawby Junction with additional MGR empties from West Burton Power Station to Immingham on 3 March 2001. (MF)

Defying the cold weather to capture Class 56s at work, No. 56096 is photographed thundering through Barnetby at the sharp end of the Scunthorpe Steelworks to Immingham MGR empties on 14 December 2001. (MF)

There was opportunity to capture a Grid in darkness at Barnetby on 14 December 2001, so the tripod was quickly set up as Transrail No. 56072 paused for a crew change while working the 6V31 Immingham to Swansea Burrows MGR empties. (MF)

During the EWS era, visits to the Southern were extremely rare but not unknown. One loco that did escape was No. 56111, which made it all the way to Marchwood on 12 September 2002 with the MOD train. The Grid would have worked the 6O12 Wagonload service from Carlisle to Eastleigh South from either Bescot or Warrington and would have then tripped the MOD portion forwards from Eastleigh Yard. This train is the 6V38 from Marchwood to Didcot, seen passing Redbridge, which would call at Eastleigh Yard en route to have more wagons added. (SC)

No. 56063 suffered from a graffiti attack and was hastily re-painted in a different version of the two-tone grey livery. The former *Bardon Hill* is seen at Newport during a crew change, working the 6B48 Trostre to Doncaster on 22 February 2002. (SC)

Routed onto the slow line at Thorne Junction, No. 56072 approaches Hatfield & Stainforth with the 6M07 Roxby to Pendleton binliner on 25 April 2002. (MF)

Coming off the freight-only line at Stainforth Junction, a Transrail Grid in the form of No. 56070 goes round the back of Hatfield & Stainforth station with the 6D86 Selby to Immingham cargowaggon van empties on 25 April 2002. (MF)

As the Class 56 pool got smaller, the locos were able to be concentrated on regular work and diagrams. One such example was the out and back steel working from Lackenby to Scunthorpe. No. 56056 is seen passing the loading bunker at Hatfield Colliery with the 6N30 loaded steel to Lackenby via Tees Yard on 13 March 2002. (SC)

There are several vantage points along the line from Brocklesby to Barnetby to view passing trains but none as iconic as the Singleton Birch Limestone & Chalk Works at Melton Ross. No. 56069 *Wolverhampton Steel Terminal* takes another load of coal to Scunthorpe on 17 June 2002. (SC)

No. 56115 was named *Barry Needham* in January 2002 in memory of the EWS controller killed in the Great Heck rail crash the year before. The loco screams towards New Barnetby with empty HAAs that are headed to Immingham Bulk 1 coal terminal for a re-fill on 21 August 2002. (SC)

Until No. 56104 was reinstated, No. 56134 *Blyth Power* was the only loco still in operation wearing Trainload coal decals. Working another regular Grid turn, No. 56134 turns on the power as it leaves Hatfield & Stainforth behind with the 6M07 Roxby to Pendleton refuse empties on 17 June 2002. (SC)

Dutch-liveried No. 56046 shatters the peace at Hatfield & Stainforth with the 6J48 loaded steel train from Scunthorpe to Aldwarke near Rotherham on 19 June 2002. (SC)

No. 56049 approaches Thorne Junction with a disappointing load forming the 6D95 Doncaster to Goole trip working on 5 April 2002. This train also usually conveyed steel products for the Goole area and could load up to a dozen wagons, the return working back to Doncaster later that day having a far healthier load. In the background is Hatfield Colliery, which hit the headlines in 2013 when the slag heap fractured and caused a landslide onto the railway line, which was closed for several months while repairs took place. (SC)

No. 56109 works hard to keep its empty MGRs on the move at New Barnetby on the climb up to Melton Ross on 21 August 2002. This loco became one of only two Grids that ran in service with one of its 'LOADHAUL' stickers missing, the other being Romanian machine No. 56027. (SC)

I was extremely lucky to capture this working on film at New Barnetby as it was late! No. 56105 has a healthy load of steel sections on tow on BDA wagons with OCA 'spacers' on the 6C49 Scunthorpe to Immingham when captured on 21 August 2002. The product will be exported to the near Continent through the port of Immingham. (SC)

Let's do the time warp again with semaphores in abundance and a banger blue loco up front. Romanian Grid No. 56006 thuds through Barnetby, making light work of the Scunthorpe Steelworks to Immingham MGR empties on 15 November 2002. (MF)

The steelworks at Scunthorpe quite often generated trip workings to and from Immingham depending on demand. One such trip working was an early evening 6G51 taking BDAs to Scunthorpe, and a de-named No. 56074 is seen on this working running several hours early on 8 July 2002. (SC)

Towards the end of its working life, No. 56056 gained a rather smoky engine, which was great from a photographic perspective but not so good for its Paxman power unit! Illustrating its ability to 'clag' nicely, No. 56056 is seen powering upgrade towards Barnetby with the 6Z22 Ripple Lane to Immingham empty newsprint vans on 9 July 2002. (SC)

The monstrosity of the new footbridge installed at Barnetby has its advantages, including providing this view of No. 56065 passing Barnetby East Signal Box with an Immingham to Scunthorpe Steelworks MGR on 25 April 2002. (MF)

Scunthorpe Steelworks received a daily trainload of coke from the ore terminal at Redcar and the load was conveyed in the distinctive HEA hoppers. Coke was used in the steelmaking industry due to the carbon monoxide produced by its combustion, which reduced iron oxides in the smelting procedure for iron ore, hence the requirement for it on a daily basis. No. 56049 passes South Bank at Teesside with the 6D78 Redcar to Scunthorpe on 3 April 2002. (SC)

EWS-liveried No. 56037 applies the power to get 6P60, the Tees Yard tripper, on the move with acid tanks destined for Seal Sands, passing through Thornaby on 19 August 2002. (MF)

Another regular Class 56 working involved moving containers for the Hoyer Group between Tees Dock and Workington via Carlisle along with acid tanks from Seal Sands. The Tees Dock to Carlisle working usually ran under the cover of darkness; however, two of the authors were present to capture No. 56087 *ABP Port of Hull* in daylight hours with the 6M57 from Tees Yard conveying just the acid tanks on 19 October 2002. It was unsure if this was that day's working running several hours early or the previous night's train running very late! (SC)

A scene captured on 30 March 2003 of Romanian No. 56018 and No. 60091 *An Teallach* resting over the weekend outside the disused sheds at Healey Mills. Unfortunately, due to the downturn in freight and the restructuring of the DB Schenker workforce, the driver depot finally closed in 2012. (MF)

Healey Mills Yard was used as a staging point for several trains at weekends. On 30 March 2003 No. 56069 *Wolverhampton Steel Terminal* basks in the sun with a rake of empty MEAs, which will go forward as 6G40 to Immingham on Monday morning for loading with coal for either Ketton or Clitheroe. (SC)

Waiting for the 'dummy' to gain access to Tees Yard, No. 56111 *Nelson* arrives at Thornaby with the 6N91 from Thrislington conveying containerised lime on 28 February 2003. (MF)

Double Loadhaul Grids are seen at Thornaby Depot on 30 March 2003, with recently stored No. 56085 awaiting its fate while classmate No. 56111, which has just been through the loco wash, is awaiting its next turn of duty. (MF)

To save money on re-painting locos, Transrail decided to put their big 'T' transfer over the previous livery, such as with Dutch-liveried No. 56049, which is seen on Teesside approaching Grangetown with the 6N21 Wilton Works to Redcar empty MGR on 31 March 2003. Two other Grids also received the big 'T' on Dutch livery – Nos 56036 and 56047. (SC)

Grangetown is situated in the shadow of the huge Lackenby Steelworks on Teesside, and also at the entrance to Tees Dock. Here, all trains on the circuit from Boulby Mine can be viewed as the trains heading for Tees Dock with potash for export run round in sidings near the signal box. In this view, No. 56103 *Stora* is on the main line with 6F78, the empty rock salt wagons from Middlesbrough Goods via a reversal in Tees Yard, on 2 April 2003. (SC)

The driver of No. 56033 *Shotton Paper Mill* climbs back into the cab before departing from Grangetown with 6F76, the empty potash wagons from Tees Dock for the mine at Boulby, on 2 April 2003. Three Class 56s were regularly diagrammed for these trains due to the volume of potash that went for export through Tees Dock. The only downside was that the 56s could only haul a trailing load of ten loaded wagons due to the gradients on the Boulby line. This increased to fifteen wagons when Class 66s took over in September 2003. (SC)

Looking rather clean in EWS livery, No. 56058 snakes its way across from Shell Junction at Grangetown having originated from Boulby Mine on the Cleveland coast with a loaded potash train destined for Tees Dock on 31 March 2003. (MF)

Double Grids at Grangetown as No. 56067 arrives with the MGR empties from Wilton while No. 56071, having run round, forms the Tees Dock–Boulby trip with a rake of Nacco potash wagons on 4 August 2003. (MF)

With bodyside battle scars and the partial loss of the Transrail decal, No. 56129 makes a fine sight rounding the Cleveland coastline at Hunts Cliff, conveying potash from Boulby Mine and heading for Tees Dock on 23 January 2003. (MF)

Like the Scunthorpe coal traffic, the potash and rock salt workings to and from Boulby on the Cleveland coast were predominantly the territory of Class 56s. There was also a daily steel trip along the branch to the then Corus-owned works at Skinningrove. Despite only having seven loaded BDAs in tow, No. 56032 gives some great audio as it rounds Hunts Cliff with the 6F46 to Tees Yard on 22 July 2003. (SC)

A working that I only saw twice on my visits to Humberside was a 'Z' working of containerised coal to Warrington Arpley. Fortunately, the second time I saw this working it was Grid-hauled and the sun was out! No. 56054 makes a splendid sight as it passes Barnetby East Signal Box on a gorgeous summer's evening in August 2003. (SC)

With the route set out of the yard onto the main, the driver needed no invitation to get the power down as No. 56051 duly delivers, passing Scunthorpe with the 6M07 Roxby to Pendleton binliner on 6 August 2003. (MF)

With the coal-handling plant of Scunthorpe Steelworks in the background, Romanian No. 56018 leaves a smoky trail as it snakes across onto the Flixborough branch with the D55 tripper conveying steel for the nearby Dragonby exchange sidings on 6 August 2003. (MF)

It is not very often that you can capture three 56s in the same frame, but fortunately for the photographer Loadhaul No. 56118 was signal checked at Scunthorpe with the 6D65 Doncaster Belmont to Immingham Enterprise on 6 August 2003. Alongside was No. 56105 on Scunthorpe coal duties while No. 56018 would later work D55/6N30 steel. (MF)

On 2 October 2003, No. 56006 gets its empty HAAs on the move from Scunthorpe after they have been discharged in the nearby coal-handling plant. Most days would see four Class 56s allocated to Scunthorpe coal diagrams, such were the vast tonnages of coal required by the blast furnaces at the steelworks, with ten loaded trains per day booked to run. The only exception to this coincided with the summer shutdown of the steelworks, making Barnetby a lot quieter with no coal or ore trains heading for Scunny. (SC)

Even as late as September 2002, No. 56104 made a surprise but welcome return to traffic to cover Class 66 diagrams as the GMs were required elsewhere for the seasonal demand for coal traffic – something that would have suited No. 56104 down to the ground given the livery it still carried! No. 56104 curves off the Roxby branch with the 6M07 empty refuse containers for Pendleton on 16 October 2003. (SC)

BR blue-liveried No. 56006 sparkles in the sun as it gets a long 6N30 Scunthorpe to Lackenby on the move from Trent Yard on 16 October 2003. No. 56058 can be seen in the background, waiting to head empty MGRs back to Immingham Bulk Terminal for re-loading. (SC)

Oil traffic from the Humber refineries also generated traffic to the local power stations in the Aire Valley, plus West Burton near Worksop and Aberthaw in Wales. These were carried in distinctive TEA tanks, as seen here when No. 56062 approaches Scunthorpe with the 6D42 Eggborough to Lindsey discharged tanks on 2 October 2003. (SC)

With the dark rain clouds giving off some peculiar lighting, No. 56103 *Stora* chases the sun with a rake of pig shed steel wagons forming the 6D89 Scunthorpe to Rotherham steel through Hatfield & Stainforth on 20 October 2003. (MF)

The last rays of sun illuminate the bodyside of Loadhaul Grid No. 56090 at Worlaby Carrs with a rake of cargowaggon vans forming the 6E33 Knowsley to Immingham Enterprise on 16 October 2003. (MF)

The border city of Carlisle was always a good place to see Class 56s, with several regular diagrams producing Grids. One such working was this infrastructure working moving engineering wagons between Kingmoor Yard, Crewe Basford Hall and Bescot. On 4 June 2003, No. 56069 *Wolverhampton Steelworks* crosses the pointwork to the south of Carlisle station with the 6C02 from Basford Hall, which has traversed the Settle and Carlisle line. The Class 56 would then head south again at lunchtime with the 6K05 to Basford Hall. (SC)

No. 56065 approaches Dalston on 23 October 2003, working the 6C48 Workington Dock to Carlisle Yard train conveying two acid tanks and a rake of flat wagons loaded with containers from the Hoyer group. The same loco would then run round its train in Carlisle Yard and head for Tees Dock as the 6E62 Enterprise. (SC)

A battle-scarred No. 56100 could be heard coming long before it was seen as it thunders through the Howgill Fells at Beck Foot with the 6K05 Carlisle Yard to Basford Hall engineers' train, formed of a long rake of loaded MLAs, on 23 October 2003. (SC)

An extremely rare working manifested itself on 13 October 2003 thanks to a Class 66 failure! The only spare loco available at Westbury was No. 56081, which was due to head light engine to Newport but instead found itself at the head of the 7O41 Westbury to Eastleigh engineers' train. It is seen here passing Millbrook near Southampton. (SC)

On 9 January 2004, having arrived at the wrong bridge only to see the familiar headlight formation of a Class 56 approaching, a mad dash in the car was made and we arrived only just in time to capture No. 56088 heading north at Raskelf on the ECML with the 6N30 Scunthorpe to Lackenby steel. (MF)

With a light covering of snow at Pontefract Monkhill, No. 56115 climbs up the incline from the Prince of Wales Colliery with a rake of short wheelbase tanks forming the 6G44 Seal Sands to Ferrybridge Power Station on 25 February 2004. (MF)

No. 56078 was an unexpected visitor to Eastleigh during 2003 and this was to show the loco to representatives of French infrastructure company Fertis. This led to several examples of Classes 56 and 58 being sent abroad from 2005 to work engineers' trains for construction of a TGV line from Paris to Strasbourg. No. 56078 passes the unusual location of Fareham with an engineers' train for a possession near Hook on 31 January 2004. (SC)

Under threatening skies, No. 56038 *Pathfinder Railtours* sweeps round the curve at Cargo Fleet station on 7 January 2004 with the 6N47 Tees Dock to Tees Yard Hoya containers, which will later form part of the 6M57 to Carlisle. (MF)

In a very smoky departure from Healey Mills, No. 56071 clears her throat through Horbury cutting with the 6D78 Neville Hill to Lindsey fuel tanks on 2 March 2004. (MF)

At the end of January 2004 I went north to Teesside in the knowledge that heavy snow was forecast for the area and I was not to be disappointed. No. 56088 passes a very wintery West Rounton with the late-running 6G50 Seal Sands to West Burton tanks on 28 January 2004. (SC)

With only a matter of days left before being switched off, No. 56078 sits in the reception road at Peterborough with the 4D56 Biggleswade to Heck empty Plasmor train on 29 March 2004. (SC)

When EWS announced that the Class 56s would be surplus to requirements by the end of March 2004, a hastily arranged railtour was organised by Pathfinder. Under the lights of Bristol Temple Meads, No. 56115 *Barry Needham* waits for time with the 1Z56 'Twilight Grids' farewell railtour on 31 March 2004. (MF)

After No. 56115 *Barry Needham* arrived at York with the 'Twilight Grid' farewell railtour, it gave way to No. 56078 *Doncaster Enterprise* for a mini tour around the Pennines. The large logo Grid is seen passing Addingford near Healey Mills with the 1Z57 York to York via Dewsbury and Stalybridge on 31 March 2004. (SC)

All was looking good for large logo No. 56078 *Doncaster Enterprise* to depart York with 1Z58 on the final leg of the railtour back to Bristol, but due to issues with the multiple jumper cable the loco was swapped for No. 56115 *Barry Needham*. (MF)

Hopes of seeing 56s back on the main line took a twist when Jarvis announced they were entering into the locomotive hire business. Enter Fastline Freight! With the locos based at Roberts Road Depot in Doncaster, a fleet of three Grids were put to work on container trains to Thamesport. No. 56302 (ex-No. 56124) and No. 56303 (ex-No. 56125) take a rest at their home depot in between turns. (SC)

Having lost interest in the freight scene since the end of the Grids in 2004, a visit to Old Oak Common was organised by my work colleague and fellow Grid man Steve Clark to photograph the stored 56s that worked abroad in France under Fertis. Captured in the glorious autumn sunshine, No. 56032 stands at the head of a long line of Grids awaiting their fate on 12 October 2008. (MF)

It was not all bad news for some of these 56s at Old Oak Common. At the time of writing, Fertis-liveried No. 56051 has had a reprieve under the ownership of Colas Rail and has recently been repainted into Colas livery at Washwood Heath before being moved to the new depot at East Crofton, Nottinghamshire. 12 October 2008. (MF)

Fastline introduced Nos 56301, 56302 and 56303 in 2005, but the company only lasted five years as they ceased trading in 2010. No. 56302 in Fastline livery has charge of the Mondays and Thursdays-only 4O90, the 10.44 Doncaster to Thamesport intermodal, which is seen approaching Water Orton on 17 July 2008. No. 56302 was originally numbered 56124. (JD)

Double Grids under the wires of the WCML at Ashton with the ghastly-looking No. 56312 (ex-No. 56003) leading sister No. 56311 (ex-No. 56057) with the 4Z91 Dollands Moor to Hams Hall 'Norfolk' liner. 10 September 2009. (MF)

Grid returnees to the main line would not be confined to the Fastline examples, as Hanson Traction also entered the fray, first with No. 56311 (ex-No. 56057) and then No. 56312 (ex-No. 56003), and it is the latter that is seen here passing Kensington Olympia with its garish 'ARTEMIS' vinyls at the head of the 4Z91 Dollands Moor to Hams Hall intermodal on 29 October 2009. (SC)

The May 2011 Swanage Diesel Gala was a landmark event for the Class 56 Group, with its newly purchased loco making its first passenger runs in preservation. In truly spectacular style, No. 56301 'clears its throat' as it leaves Corfe Castle behind in a cloud of clag with a Norden to Swanage service. (SC)

In a location now consigned to history with the electrification of the GWML, DCR-liveried No. 56311 (ex-No. 56057) approaches Moreton with the short-lived 6Z48 Thornley Mill to Calvert Crossrail spoil on 5 June 2013. (MF)

A four-hour round trip just for one shot, but DCR No. 56303 (ex-No. 56125) duly delivers in some cracking evening light as she approaches Hinksey with the 6Z92 Didcot Power Station to Calvert flyash on 30 April 2013. (MF)

DCR were another small operator that took on some 56s for the locomotive 'spot hire' market. They soon gained some regular work based at Totton near Southampton where a top and tailed 'Railvac' train would travel around the Wessex area tackling wet spots on the track during night-time possessions. Therefore, a wagon move was required to get the rolling stock into place and No. 56312 is seen passing Old Dilton with a 6Z56 Long Marston to Totton Yard on 20 September 2013. The loco had recently been repainted in DCR colours and named *Jeremiah Dixon (Son of County Durham, Surveyor of the Mason–Dixon Line USA.* (SC)

No. 56303 is passing through Oxford with the 6Z91 Calvert to Didcot Power Station empty flyash wagons on 13 March 2013. The loco is in DCR green livery and is operated by British American Railway Services (BARS) and based at Washwood Heath. It was originally built as No. 56125. (JD)

Fine weather and a loco change on the flyash diagram, plus a three-hour round trip to Culham, allows the capturing of unbranded Fertis-liveried No. 56091 powering the 6Z92 Didcot Power Station to Calvert flyash on 22 May 2013. (MF)

The sound of a 56 on full chat is something to behold as Colas Rail No. 56302 (ex-No. 56124) thuds past the gallery at Undy with the 6Z53 Teigngrace to Chirk logs on 11 July 2013. (MF)

Colas picked up a lot of the ex-Fertis Grids for their first dip into the UK freight market, and one of these examples, No. 56105, approaches Warrington Bank Quay on 16 August 2013 with the 6Z70 Ribblehead to Chirk loaded log train. (SC)

Colas No. 56105 is passing the Hinksey Reservoir with the 6Z56 Crewe to West Ealing on 10 June 2013. (JD)

With the sun dipping below the hills and the lengthening shadows behind me, it was a very close call before losing the light completely but in the nick of time No. 56078 and No. 56113 driven by Nigel Miles aka 'Flub' pass through the Wylye valley at Stockon with the 6Z29 Eastleigh to Westbury engineers' on 11 January 2014. (MF)

It is rush-hour on the M1 motorway in the background as No. 56094 makes light work of twenty canvas-covered wagons as it rounds the sweeping curve at Lockington with the 6E07 Washwood Heath to Boston steel empties on 1 July 2014. (MF)

A scene now impossible to recreate due to the electrification of the GWML sees No. 56312 on the Up fast at Moreton Cutting near Didcot with a 5Z56 stock move from Bristol Barton Hill to Chiltern's Wembley Depot, conveying an overhauled Mark 3 carriage and a DVT on 26 February 2014. (SC)

The 5Z57 Totton Yard to Eastleigh is at Mount Pleasant level crossing, Southampton, with No. 56301 leading and No. 56303 on the rear on 2 June 2014. No. 56301 was originally numbered 56045 before being taken over by Fastline, whose livery it is still wearing. Now, however, it is part of the UK Rail Leasing fleet. (JD)

With the sun dodging the clouds, No. 56113 passes a field of rapeseed at Bourton with the lightly loaded 6V62 Tilbury to Llanwern steel empties on 7 May 2014. (MF)

An early start was needed to capture the overnight Railvac operations returning to their base at Totton, and at just gone 6.30 a.m., No. 56311 leads classmate No. 56301 with the 6Z41 St Margarets to Totton at Eastleigh on 12 June 2014. Thankfully the Up passenger train cleared just in time! (SC)

Colas No. 56105 is seen passing Tamworth High Level station with 6E07, the 14.50 Washwood Heath to Boston steel wagons, on 30 May 2014. (JD)

Another short-term contract was for Colas to move steel between Llanwern and Newport Docks. Hooded steel wagons were brought out of storage at Long Marston and moved to Wales for this flow and a short rake of these form the 6Z42 from Newport Docks to Llanwern, which is seen passing East Usk Yard at Somerton with No. 56302 and No. 56087 at the business end on 3 September 2014. (SC)

No. 56113 is heading west towards Salisbury when seen at Lockerley with 6Z29, the 11.46 Eastleigh to Westbury, on 3 January 2014. (JD)

No. 56312 carries the very lengthy name of *Jeremiah Dixon Son of County Durham Surveyor of the Mason–Dixon Line USA*. It was originally numbered 56003 and is top and tailed with No. 56103 on the 6Y57 07.20 Weymouth to Totton Yard Railvac. It is seen near Beaulieu Road in the New Forest on 31 August 2014. (JD)

No. 56311 was originally numbered 56057; it is seen here at Southampton with the 6Z34 10.30 Totton Yard to Chaddesden on 22 August 2014. (JD)

Due to a sudden upturn in value of scrap metal, a short-term flow ran from the north-east of England to South Wales. No. 56103 thuds through Severn Tunnel Junction with the return 6Z35 Cardiff Tidal to Stockton scrap empties on 17 February 2015. (MF)

DCR operated several trains of spoil from Willesden to the huge landfill site at Calvert in Buckinghamshire and Class 56s made a welcome return to the Chiltern lines, having last been seen on containerised refuse trains heading for Calvert. No. 56312 is passing the tranquil setting of Denham with the 6Z57 Calvert to Willesden Euro Terminal, towing a lengthy rake of JRA bogie box wagons on 10 June 2015. (SC)

A short-term hire of DCR traction for the movement of coaching stock on behalf of Chiltern Railways sees No. 56104 passing Callow Hill with the 5Z35 Wembley to Bristol Barton Hill ECS move on 24 February 2016. (MF)

Nos 56104 and 56081 are owned and operated by UK Rail Leasing and are in the early Railfreight grey livery without any of the British Rail markings. They are seen running about eighty minutes early at Creech St Michael with the 5S56 10.53 Plymouth Laira to Kilmarnock HST coaches on 4 March 2016. (JD)

UK Rail Leasing's No. 56081 is at Cossington on 24 June 2016 with the 6Z35 11.35 Shipley Crossley Evans to Cardiff Tidal bogie scrap wagons. This was the first UKRL loco to work on the main line, in 2014. (JD)

In a surprise development, the 2016 railhead treatment train season saw Colas being awarded two core routes – one based at Gloucester and the other at Shrewsbury for the North Wales coast. While the Shrewsbury circuit Class 56s generally ran well, there were a few problems with the Gloucester-based locos. On 7 November 2016, No. 56078 was 'failed' with severe wheelflats and dumped at Worcester. While No. 56105 continued with some of the circuit, a replacement was sent for in the form of ROG No. 56104. In glorious autumnal light the pair head the 3S34 Gloucester to Gloucester past Croome Perry, only to fail a couple of miles down the track in Ashchurch loop. The Grids were hastily replaced by Freightliner 66s for the rest of the 2016 RHTT season. (SC)

Thanks to Gen from the Headsup Group, a short journey was made to capture No. 56078. With a sole Railvac in tow, it is seen passing Fairwood with the 6X54 Plymouth to Westbury on 25 September 2016. (MF)

One of the first occasions a main line FOC loco worked at the annual Swanage Diesel Gala was in fact at the most recent, in 2017. Colas sent recently overhauled No. 56096 to Dorset and the loco sparkles in the spring sunshine as it is seen passing Townsend Bridge with the 16.45 Swanage to Norden on 7 May 2017. On arrival at Norden, the Grid was swiftly detached and sent light engine back to Eastleigh. (SC)

# About the Authors

**John Dedman** – John has lived in the New Forest area all his life and railways were in the blood, with both his grandfather and father having railway-associated jobs based around Lymington. Going to school in Brockenhurst, trains were a welcome distraction during break times and probably during lessons as well! John's interest in photography was rekindled when his first marital home was near the railway line in New Milton. John has been fortunate enough to travel the length and breadth of the country and his camera was always close by. This has allowed John to publish several books with Noodle Books and Amberley Publishing on various aspects of British Rail rolling stock. John is also a member of a small photographic group, which is where he met Mark and Steve and the idea for this book was born. https://www.flickr.com/photos/johndedman/

**Steve Clark** – Steve blames his grandparents for his love of trains, as staying with them during school summer holidays always led to a trip out by train somewhere on the 'Southern'. A chance trip to his local WH Smiths in Farnham found him purchasing his first ABC locomotive numbers book, but it was not until he was sixteen that he really began to fill up the book with 'Cops', having joined the Railway Enthusiasts Society Ltd, which organised visits around depots and works with permits. Steve got his dream job in 1995 when he joined the railway working as a guard, initially based at Guildford, then Farnham and finally Bournemouth. A chance meeting in the Midlands in 1998 with fellow author Mark Finch led to an instant friendship that still remains today, and many miles were covered by the pair chasing Class 56s around the country before their demise in 2004. https://www.flickr.com/photos/131175774@N06/

**Mark Finch** – Career railwayman Mark joined BR on the YTS scheme back in the late 1980s and has never looked back. Taking advantage of the free travel as a perk of the job meant that Mark travelled far and wide on spotting trips and it was from those trips that his love of Class 56s became apparent. During a chance meeting in 1998 at Stenson Junction with Steve it was discussed how the 56s were surplus to requirements as the 'future' in the form of Class 66s passed by in a convoy heading for Toton Open Day. The race was then on to record the class in action. Mark has a good eye for a photograph and also some superb processing has led to some great images for the book. Mark spends a lot of his spare time tending for and riding his horse, but the camera is never far away. https://www.flickr.com/photos/gridchaser/

# Bibliography

Books

*British Railways Locomotives & Coaching Stock,* various editions (Platform 5 Publishing Ltd).
Bulmer, Keith, *Grids: The Class 56 Story*
Clough, David N., *Locomotive Profile: Type 5 Freight Diesels*


Magazine

*Rail Express Magazine*


Websites

Class 56 Group website: www.class56group.co.uk
Freightmaster Forums